FROM SEA to SHINING SEA

COLORADO

AMY MILLER

Consultants

MELISSA N. MATUSEVICH, PH.D.
Curriculum and Instruction Specialist
Blacksburg, Virginia

KIM R. MEYER
Library Information Specialist
Marshdale Elementary
Evergreen, Colorado

CHILDREN'S PRESS ®
AN IMPRINT OF SCHOLASTIC INC.

New York • Toronto • London • Auckland • Sydney • Mexico City
New Delhi • Hong Kong • Danbury, Connecticut

Colorado is in the southwestern part of the United States. It is bordered by Utah, Wyoming, Nebraska, Kansas, Oklahoma, and New Mexico.

Project Editor: Meredith DeSousa
Art Director: Marie O'Neill
Photo Researcher: Marybeth Kavanagh
Design: Robin West, Ox and Company, Inc.
Page 6 map and recipe art: Susan Hunt Yule
All other maps: XNR Productions, Inc.

Library of Congress Cataloging-in-Publication Data

Miller, Amy.
    Colorado / by Amy Miller.
      p. cm. - (From sea to shining sea)
    Includes bibliographical references and index.
    ISBN-13: 978-0-531-20802-1
    ISBN-10: 0-531-20802-8
    1. Colorado-Juvenile literature. I. Title. II. Series.

F776.3 .M55 2008
978.8—dc22
                               2007046534

TABLE of CONTENTS

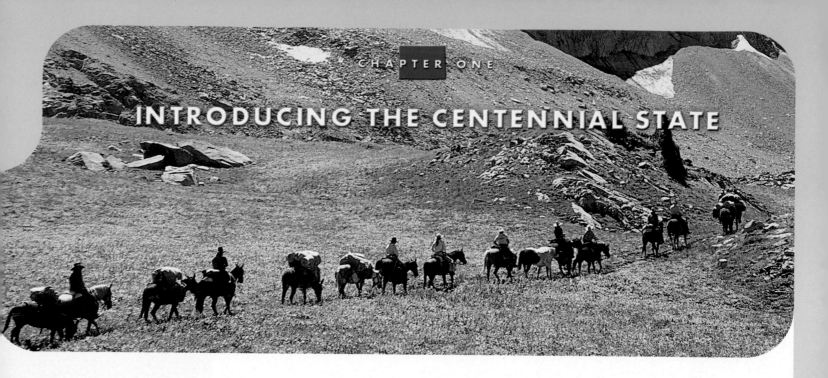

CHAPTER ONE

INTRODUCING THE CENTENNIAL STATE

Many people prefer traveling on horseback to get a close-up view of the Rocky Mountains.

Colorado is the eighth largest state in the country. All of the six New England states (Massachusetts, Connecticut, Maine, Vermont, New Hampshire, and Rhode Island) put together would fit inside Colorado's borders, with lots of room to spare.

Early explorers from Mexico gave Colorado its name. It means "red-colored" in Spanish and was named after the Colorado River, which flows through red-colored rock called sandstone. Colorado's official nickname is the Centennial State because it became a state in 1876, when the United States celebrated the one hundredth anniversary, or centennial, of the Declaration of Independence.

Nestled in the heart of the Rocky Mountains, Colorado is a place of scenic wonders. The Rocky Mountains are an important part of Colorado's history. In the nineteenth century, rough-and-tumble pioneers came to Colorado hoping to strike it rich by mining gold or silver in the mountains.

Today, thousands of people still come to Colorado. They come to enjoy some of the world's best ski slopes. Others come to camp, hike, fish, or just relax and enjoy the scenery. There's something for everyone in Colorado, whether you enjoy the outdoors or are interested in learning about our country's exciting and colorful frontier past.

What comes to mind when you think of Colorado?

* Stegosaurus and Tyrannosaurus rex roaming the plains millions of years ago
* Native American tribes hunting buffalo
* United States Army Lieutenant Zebulon Pike exploring the Rocky Mountains
* Gold and silver miners hoping to strike it rich
* Cowboys driving herds of cattle across the plains
* Companies building rockets for space travel
* The Denver Broncos winning the Super Bowl
* Skiers gliding down snow-covered mountains
* Young men and women training to be Air Force officers at the U.S. Air Force Academy

Colorado means many things to many people. In this book, you'll read about the people and places that helped develop the Centennial State. You'll discover the story of Colorado.

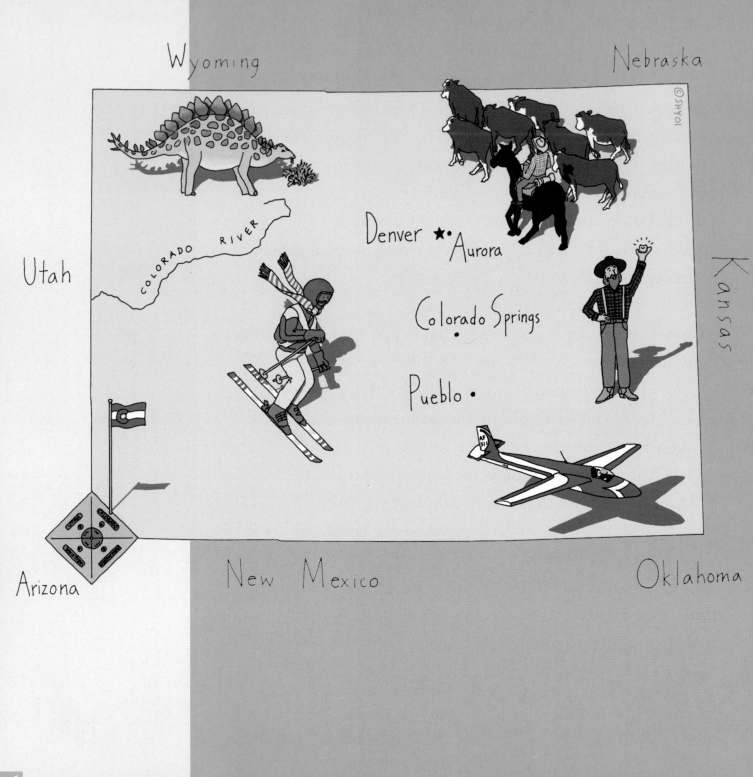

Wyoming

Nebraska

Utah

COLORADO RIVER

Denver ★ •Aurora

Colorado Springs
•

Pueblo •

Kansas

Arizona

New Mexico

Oklahoma

6

CHAPTER TWO

THE LAND OF COLORADO

If you look on a map, you'll see that Colorado is a big rectangle in the center of the western United States. It is the eighth largest state in the country, covering 104,094 square miles (269,601 square kilometers).

Colorado is one of the few states whose boundaries are not defined by a natural feature, such as a river or a mountain. Wyoming and part of Nebraska form Colorado's northern boundary. Parts of Nebraska and Kansas lie to the east. Oklahoma and New Mexico are to the south, and Utah is to the west. Arizona touches Colorado's southwest corner. In fact, this boundary is the only place in the United States where four states—Colorado, Utah, New Mexico, and Arizona—meet. At Four Corners Monument, you can put each hand and foot in a different state!

Hiking is one of the best ways to explore the mountainous landscape of western Colorado.

Colorado has three major land regions: the Rocky Mountains, the Great Plains, and the Colorado Plateau.

THE ROCKY MOUNTAINS

The Rocky Mountains begin in Canada and run southward toward Mexico, passing through the west central part of Colorado. The Colorado Rockies are part of the southern Rocky Mountains.

Five major mountain ranges sweep through Colorado. They are the Front Range, the Sangre de Cristo ("Blood of Christ") Range, the Sawatch Range, the Park Range, and the San Juan Mountains. Rocky Mountain National Park is located where the Front Range and Medicine Bow Mountains meet in north central Colorado.

Although the Rocky Mountains cover only one-third of Colorado, they are Colorado's most prominent natural feature. Some people call the Colorado Rockies "the Roof of North America" because more than fifty peaks rise above 14,000 feet (4,267 meters). The tallest mountain in Colorado is Mount Elbert, at 14,433 feet (4,399 m). Located in the Sawatch Mountains, it is the second-highest peak in the 48 contiguous United States. Overall, Colorado has the highest average altitude in the United States—about 6,800 feet (2,073 m), or higher than one mile (1.6 kilometers).

If you drew a line on a map along the highest ridge line of the Colorado Rockies, you would be roughly tracing the Continental Divide. Rivers east of the divide flow into the Mississippi River system, which

Colorado's many mountain ranges provide a scenic backdrop to the landscape. The San Juan Mountains are shown here.

empties into the Gulf of Mexico. Rivers west of the divide flow into the Pacific Ocean.

There are many types of trees in the Colorado Rockies. Only firs, spruces, and pines can survive the fierce winds and cold temperatures on the highest mountains. In the lower elevations, piñon pine, juniper, aspen, cottonwood, and maple trees grow. In the fall, the shimmering green leaves of Aspen trees turn golden and color the mountainsides. In spring and summer, wildflowers blanket the mountain meadows.

Yankee Boy Basin, near Ouray, has one of the best wildflower displays in all of Colorado.

Many animals make their home in the Rocky Mountains. Mountain goats and bighorn sheep are the only animals strong enough to live high in the mountains. Bears, deer, elk, mountain lions, squirrels, and other small animals live along the slopes.

THE GREAT PLAINS

At the foot of the eastern slope of the Colorado Rockies is a stretch of flat, dry land called the Great Plains. It is a large ribbon of flat grassland about 400 miles (640 km) wide. It runs through the midwestern part of the United States, beginning in Canada and ending in southern Texas.

Bighorn sheep, Colorado's state animal, are found only in the Rocky Mountains.

In 1820, United States Army Major Stephen Long surveyed the South Platte River, one of the major rivers located in the plains. After seeing miles and miles of grass and sand dunes, he called the region "uninhabitable" and "wholly unfit for cultivation." His assistant named it the "Great American Desert."

In the 1850s, settlers traveling west heard of Major Long's reports. They

FIND OUT MORE

For many years, no one was sure how the Rocky Mountains were formed. Today, we know much more about how mountains were created. What is the scientific explanation for how the Rocky Mountains were formed?

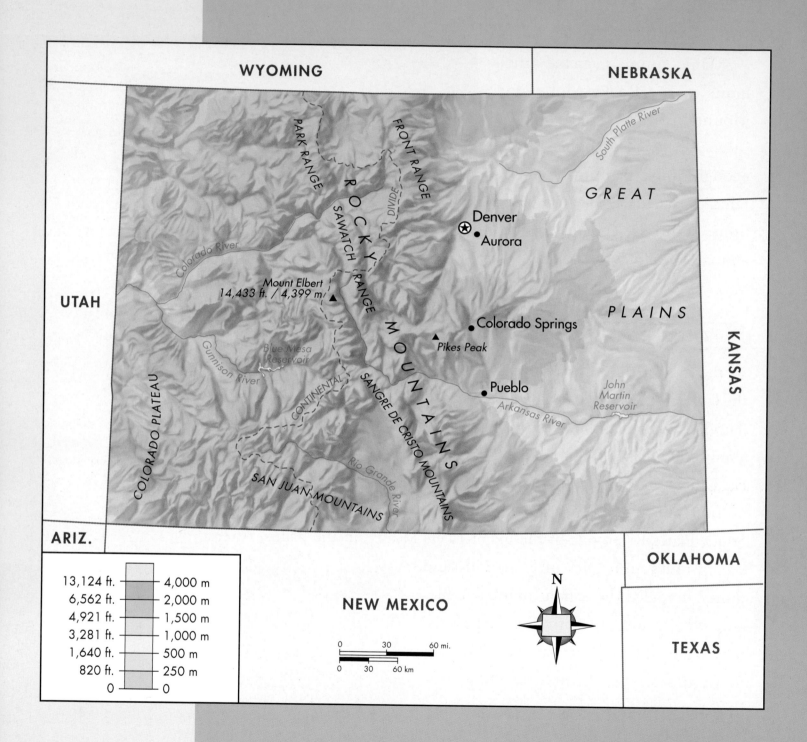

WYOMING

NEBRASKA

PARK RANGE

FRONT RANGE

ROCKY

SAWATCH RANGE

DIVIDE

South Platte River

Denver

Aurora

GREAT

UTAH

Colorado River

Mount Elbert
14,433 ft. / 4,399 m

Blue Mesa
Reservoir

Gunnison River

MOUNTAINS

Colorado Springs

Pikes Peak

PLAINS

CONTINENTAL

SANGRE DE CRISTO MOUNTAINS

Pueblo

John
Martin
Reservoir

KANSAS

COLORADO PLATEAU

SAN JUAN MOUNTAINS

Rio Grande River

Arkansas River

ARIZ.

OKLAHOMA

13,124 ft. — 4,000 m
6,562 ft. — 2,000 m
4,921 ft. — 1,500 m
3,281 ft. — 1,000 m
1,640 ft. — 500 m
820 ft. — 250 m
0 — 0

NEW MEXICO

0   30   60 mi.

0   30   60 km

N

TEXAS

thought this land would be too dry for farming, so they bypassed Colorado on their way to California. As a result, few pioneers made their homes there. Today, however, all of Colorado's major towns and cities, including Denver and Colorado Springs, are in this region.

Irrigation projects such as the Colorado-Big Thompson Project helped turn the plains into an agricultural powerhouse. Now tunnels bring water to the plains so that farmers are able to grow food such as alfalfa, oats, and rye, and also raise cattle, goats, and sheep. The region that Major Long once called the "Great American Desert" is part of a region now known as "The Breadbasket of the World" because farmers here grow much of the world's wheat.

Although the plains are dry, many animals live there. Small animals, such as jackrabbits and prairie dogs, thrive on the plains. Bird-watchers will find the state bird, the lark bunting, on the prairie. Blue jays, chickadees, and meadowlarks can also be seen.

Colorado is one of the top ten wheat-growing states in the nation.

FIND OUT MORE

The Great Plains yields more than food. The region also produces more oil than any other part of the United States. How much oil does the United States produce and use every year?

THE COLORADO PLATEAU

The western slope of the Rockies leads to the Colorado Plateau. A plateau is a high, level piece of land. Over thousands of years, the Colorado River and its smaller branches have cut deep canyons into the plateau, forming large, flat-topped hills with steep sides called mesas. Grand Mesa, between the Colorado and Gunnison Rivers, is one of the world's largest flat-topped mountains.

Mesas are found in the southwestern part of Colorado.

Millions of years ago, these mesas were covered in lush green plant life. Today, this region is mostly dry grassland with only a few trees and shrubs. There are still plenty of natural resources. Companies drill for oil and natural gas, and miners dig for coal.

Many large farms are in this region. Farmers near the town of Grand Junction are famous for growing mouthwatering peaches, as well as apples, cherries, and plums. Ranchers raise cattle and sheep. During summer, sheep herds graze on the grasslands of the mesas.

The Arkansas River winds through the mountain valleys and canyons of Colorado as well as Kansas, Oklahoma, and Arkansas.

RIVERS AND LAKES

Several of the most important rivers in the western United States begin in the mountains of Colorado. The Colorado, the Rio Grande, the Arkansas, and the Platte Rivers all begin in the Colorado Rockies. Many smaller rivers, called tributaries, feed into these rivers. They provide much-needed water to many western states.

The Colorado River is one of most important rivers in the United States. It is 1,450 miles

Many dams, such as the giant Hoover Dam, have been built on the Colorado River to harness its enormous power. How do dams turn the Colorado River's mighty current into power that people can use?

The Royal Gorge and suspension bridge are popular tourist attractions in Colorado.

(2,334 km) long and drains one-twelfth of the land in the United States. It begins in the Colorado Rockies and flows southwest to Utah. It then flows through Arizona, and finally makes its way into the Gulf of California. The river was first named Rio Colorado, which means "red-colored river," by Spanish explorers because it flows through the red-colored sandstone of the Colorado Plateau.

Some of Colorado's rivers have carved deep gorges and canyons into the landscape. The Arkansas River formed the Royal Gorge, west of Cañon City. This gorge is more than 1,000 feet (300 m) deep. The Royal Gorge Bridge, which stands 1,053 feet (321 m) above the floor of the Royal Gorge, is the highest suspension bridge in the world.

Colorado has hundreds of natural lakes, both large and small. The largest natural lake is Grand Lake, which covers one square mile (3 sq km). Dams along Colorado's rivers have also created manmade, or artificial, lakes called reservoirs. The largest manmade lakes are the John Martin Reservoir in eastern Colorado and the Blue Mesa Reservoir on the Gunnison River in western Colorado.

CLIMATE

Coloradans enjoy a mostly dry, sunny climate. However, the weather is cooler and wetter in the Rockies than it is on the plains. In summer, the average temperature in Leadville, located in the mountains, is about 55° Fahrenheit (13° Celsius). The plains are warmer, with an average temperature of 74°F (23°C). In winter, Leadville's average temperature is 18°F (–8°C), while on the plains it is 28°F (–2°C).

The mountains also get more rain than lower elevations. High mountains get about 45 inches (114 centimeters) of rain and snow each year. Colorado's eastern plains get only about 15 inches (38 cm) of rain and snow each year. The reason for this is because clouds full of moisture from the Pacific Ocean rise as they travel over the mountains. Snow and rain falls on the western slope and the central mountains, but very often the moisture is gone by the time clouds reach the eastern plains.

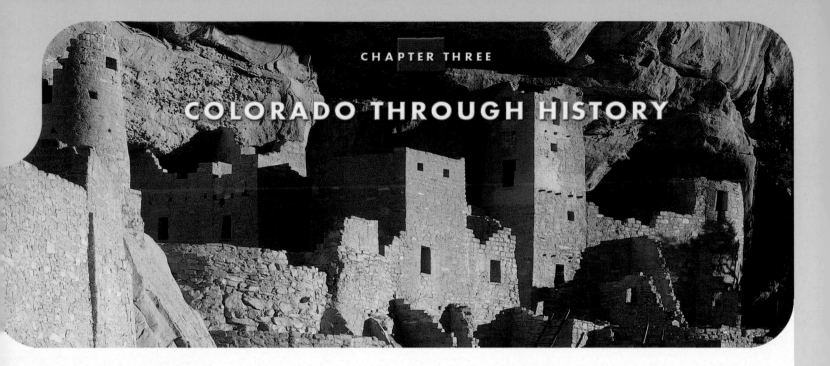

CHAPTER THREE

COLORADO THROUGH HISTORY

Cliff Palace, the largest cliff house at Mesa Verde National Park, has more than 200 rooms.

The first people arrived in the area that is today southwestern Colorado about 12,000 to 20,000 years ago. They came to North America to hunt large prehistoric elephants called mammoths. Scientists believe these people came from Asia by crossing the Bering Land Bridge, which once connected Asia with North America. Today, the majority of this land bridge lies beneath the Bering and Chukchi Seas (between Alaska and Siberia).

The next group of people who lived in the Colorado area are called Basket Makers because they weaved baskets from the long, tough spines of yucca plants. They also made beautiful pottery. The Basket Makers lived on the mesas,

EXTRA! EXTRA!

Millions of years ago, before people arrived, dinosaurs roamed Colorado. The bones of at least a dozen dinosaur species have been found there, including the plant-eating Apatosaurus, the meat-eating Tyrannosaurus rex, and the Stegosaurus. The Stegosaurus was named Colorado's state fossil in 1991.

or flat-topped mountains, of south-western Colorado before A.D. 100. As the seasons changed, they moved in search of food. They were hunters and gatherers, and they had no permanent homes.

Around A.D. 400 a new group of people called the Anasazi lived on Colorado land. Anasazi is a Navajo word that means "ancient ones." Unlike the Basket Makers, the Anasazi were farmers who lived in the same place year-round. They grew corn, squash, and beans. They also kept turkeys and weaved their feathers into warm blankets.

The Anasazi are known as Cliff Dwellers because they carved houses out of mountainsides. Some houses were as large as today's apartment buildings, with hundreds of rooms. The dry weather has helped preserve many of these dwellings, and they can be seen today at Mesa Verde National Park.

The Anasazi lived among the mountains by building homes directly into the sides of cliffs.

19

FIND OUT MORE

Scientists have studied many objects, such as baskets, bones, and bits of clothing, to learn how the Anasazi lived. How do scientists unearth artifacts from these ancient sites? What tools do they use?

The Anasazi began leaving the area around 1300, heading south and east. No one is exactly sure why they left. Scientists suspect there are many reasons. They may have been forced out by drought, a long period of dry weather. Or a hostile tribe may have invaded. Disease may also have driven the Anasazi from their homes.

The Anasazi left thousands of pictures that were carved and painted onto large stones and mountain walls. Scientists have studied these pictures to learn how the Anasazi lived.

Later, several other Native American tribes moved into Colorado. A people called the Ute lived in the mountains of western Colorado. The word Ute means "people who dwell in the tops of mountains." They hunted deer and gathered fruits and berries. The Cheyenne, Arapaho, and Comanche lived on the plains in eastern Colorado. They hunted buffalo and lived in tents called tepees, which were made of animal skins.

EUROPEAN AND AMERICAN EXPLORERS

Spanish explorers were the first Europeans to reach the area that is now Colorado. In 1540, Spaniard Francisco Vasquez de Coronado, the governor of a province in Mexico, led an expedition through Colorado. He had heard rumors that cities made of gold could be found there. Instead, he found small Native American villages.

Determined to find gold, Coronado sent one of his men, Garcia Lopez de Cardenas, to investigate further. The smaller expedition found

the Grand Canyon on the Colorado River, but they never found gold. Coronado's group left without settling the area.

French explorers also arrived there during this time. In 1682, René-Robert Cavelier, Sieur de La Salle, arrived in what is now eastern Colorado. He claimed a huge area for France and called it Louisiana, after King Louis of France.

In 1706, Spanish explorer Juan de Ulibarri explored western Colorado near what is now Pueblo. He claimed the region, which he named San Luis, for Spain. In 1776, two Spanish missionaries, or priests, were the first to explore, map, and report on the land of Colorado.

It wasn't until 1803 that eastern and central Colorado became part of the United States. In what became known as the Louisiana Purchase,

FIND OUT MORE

The Louisiana Purchase included parts of what later became thirteen separate states. Look at a map of the United States in 1803, and compare it to a map of the United States today. Which states were part of the Louisiana Purchase?

Zebulon Pike was the first American explorer to set eyes on Pikes Peak in 1806.

President Thomas Jefferson negotiated with France to buy a huge piece of land between the Mississippi River and the Rocky Mountains, which included part of Colorado. The Louisiana Purchase nearly doubled the size of the United States.

In 1806, Lieutenant Zebulon Pike and twenty-two men explored the southwestern boundary of the new territory. They wanted to find the source of the Arkansas River and the Red River. After traveling four months, they arrived in what is now Colorado and caught sight of the Rocky Mountains. One mountain peak appeared to be so high that Pike thought no one could climb it. They named the giant mountain Pikes Peak. It wasn't until 1820 that Dr. Edwin James, part of a group of explorers led by United States Army Major Stephen Long, managed to climb Pikes Peak.

FUR TRADERS AND MOUNTAIN MEN

Gradually, more people made their way to Colorado. Mountain men and fur trappers from France, Mexico, and the United States came to Colorado in the 1820s and 1830s. They came in search of beavers and other fur-bearing animals, which, at that time, were especially valuable in Europe. These furs were used to make hats and were often in great demand. In later years, the shaggy fur of the buffalo was used to make fur coats.

Many traders and pioneers came to southern Colorado from other parts of the United States by following the Santa Fe Trail. The trail began in Independence, Missouri, and ended in Santa Fe, New Mexico. In 1833, Charles and William Bent set up the first fur-trading post in Colorado on the Santa Fe Trail next to the Arkansas River. It became known as Bent's Fort and was the first permanent settlement in Colorado. The Bent brothers bought furs and buffalo pelts from trappers and Native Americans, and sent them by wagon train to St. Louis, Missouri. Famous frontiersmen such as Kit Carson traded there.

During the 1830s, Mexico claimed much of what is now the western United States, including the western part of Colorado. In the 1840s, President James K. Polk wanted to acquire the area that is now Texas from Mexico. The Mexican government, however, did not want to give up the land, so in 1846 the United States declared war on Mexico. As a result of losing the Mexican-American War (1846–1848), Mexico was forced to sell all its land north of the Rio Grande River to the United States. All of what is today Colorado was now part of the United States.

Early gold prospectors used a cradle to search for gold. The cradle had a sieve to separate gold from dirt.

In 1858, William Green Russell found gold in Cherry Creek, a tributary of the South Platte River. After his discovery, thousands of gold seekers from across the country came to Colorado in hopes of getting rich. Some of them traveled in wagons with painted signs that read "Pikes Peak or Bust."

The settlers founded two settlements where the South Platte River meets Cherry Creek. One was named Auraria, which is Latin for "gold." The other was called Denver City, named after James W. Denver, governor of the Kansas Territory. In 1860, the settlements joined together under the name Denver. Several other small towns, such as Central City and Black Hawk, were also settled.

Life wasn't easy in these settlements. Fires, floods, drought, and attacks from Native Americans were always a threat. Despite this, some rough-and-tumble mountain settlements became bustling "boom towns," towns that developed virtually overnight. Homes and stores were built, and the streets were busy with people and activity. One vis-

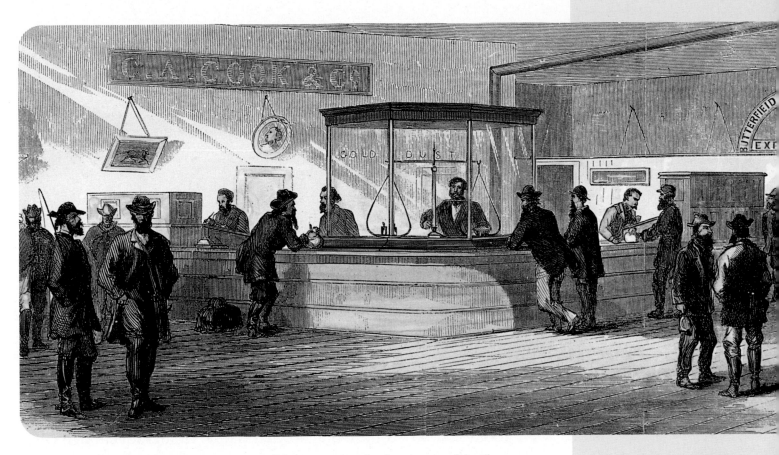

itor described the boom towns as "thriving, orderly, peaceable, busy . . . with churches and schools."

Gold was so plentiful that miners often paid for food and other supplies with "pinches" of gold dust. Because of a lack of safe, reliable transportation, it was difficult to deliver supplies to isolated cities such as Denver. Food was expensive. One egg was worth four pinches of gold dust. With sixty pinches of gold dust, miners could buy a sack of potatoes.

Men brought their gold to a banking house, where they could exchange gold dust for money.

WHO'S WHO IN COLORADO?

Clara Brown (1800–1885) was born a slave in Virginia. In 1859, she bought her freedom and traveled by wagon train to Colorado, where she established a successful laundry business in Central City. She helped other freed slaves to settle in Colorado, and founded Denver's first Sunday school. Today, the capitol building has a stained-glass window that was made in her honor.

Many women came to Colorado, too. In 1859, Elizabeth Byers founded Denver's first newspaper, the *Rocky Mountain News,* together with her husband, William Byers. Clara Brown, who arrived in 1859, was the first African-American settler in Colorado.

THE COLORADO TERRITORY

At the time of the gold rush, the land that would become Colorado was split among four United States territories—New Mexico, Utah, Kansas, and Nebraska. The territories were spread out over a large area, however, and their governments were far away. For this reason, settlers in the Colorado region wanted to create a new territory. In 1861 there were about 25,000 people living in what is now Colorado, enough people for the United States government to create the Colorado Territory. Colorado City was named its territorial capital.

The new territory soon faced conflict with Native Americans. The United States government had forced the Cheyenne and Arapaho onto a small tract of land, called a reservation, between the Arkansas River and Sand Creek. Over time, Native Americans grew angry at having their land taken away. In June 1864, tensions peaked, and the Cheyenne and a small band of warriors killed the Hungate family outside of Denver. This made white settlers even more suspicious of the Native Americans. Arapaho and Cheyenne leaders met with territorial

This drawing shows a main street in Denver in 1866.

governor John Evans hoping to negotiate a treaty (a formal agreement) that would bring peace. While they waited for a treaty to be written, about 700 Native American men, women, and children settled on Sand Creek near Fort Lyon, where they were assured of safety.

Although a peace treaty was in progress, Colonel John Chivington, leader of the Third Colorado Calvary, decided to take matters into his own hands. On November 29, 1864, he led a brutal attack on the Sand Creek Reservation. His soldiers were ordered to kill every Native American, including women and children. Between 200 and 400 Cheyenne and Arapaho were killed. Only nine Ameri-

FIND OUT MORE

Jim Beckwourth was an African American from Virginia. He came to the Rocky Mountains in the 1820s and worked at Bent's Fort as a fur trader. He discovered a pass through the Sierra Nevada Mountains that became known as Beckwourth Pass. Try to locate the pass on a map of the Sierra Nevadas.

can soldiers died in the attack. An outraged Congress called the attack "a foul and dastardly massacre which could have disgraced the veriest savages."

Native American tribes throughout the region sought revenge. They burned the town of Julesburg, Colorado, to the ground. Over the next two years, hundreds of people died in the violence that followed.

CIVIL WAR

As struggles took place in the new territory, conflicts were also going on in the rest of the country. In 1860, Abraham Lincoln was elected president. Lincoln was against slavery, a common practice in the South. Enslaved African Americans were owned by whites, who forced them to do backbreaking labor on large farms called plantations. Slaves were not allowed to marry, own property, or learn how to read and write. They were often harshly punished if they tried to escape. By 1860, four million enslaved African Americans lived in the United States.

Although slavery was illegal in the North, many Southerners depended on slavery to run their plantations. They feared that Lincoln would try to abolish (put an end to) slavery. Shortly after he was elected several southern states seceded, or withdrew, from the United States and formed a new nation called the Confederate States of America. Tension between North and South grew so high that the Civil War (1861–1865) broke out between the Union and the Confederacy.

Even though the war was mainly fought in the east, people in Colorado became involved in the war. Most Coloradans fought on the Union side because there was very little slavery in Colorado. The First Colorado Cavalry fought in New Mexico to stop Confederate soldiers from moving farther west. In 1865 the North won the war and slavery was outlawed in the United States.

In 1879, the Denver & Rio Grande Railroad won the right to lay down tracks through the Royal Gorge, which had room for only one railroad.

STATEHOOD

Shortly after the Civil War, Colorado's gold supply dwindled. Many miners left the territory to look for work elsewhere. Colorado's future looked bleak until the railroad came. Railroads helped Colorado's farmers, ranchers, and businesspeople send products all over the country. Railroads also brought many settlers to the new territory.

Building railroads over Colorado's rugged mountains wasn't easy. When the Union Pacific Railroad was built in 1869, railway developers bypassed Denver. Instead, they chose an easier route north of Colorado, through Wyoming.

In 1870, a group of Denver businessmen started the Denver Pacific Railroad, which connected Denver with Cheyenne, Wyoming. Soon after, William Jackson Palmer built the Denver & Rio Grande Railroad, connecting Denver with Colorado Springs and eventually Pueblo. The arrival of the railroad led many cities to develop almost overnight, including Pueblo, Colorado Springs, and Trinidad.

By 1876, there were 40,000 settlers living in the Colorado Territory, enough to declare statehood. On August 1, 1876, Colorado became the thirty-eighth state, just one month after the United States celebrated its centennial. From then on, Colorado was known as the "Centennial State."

William Jackson Palmer founded the Denver & Rio Grande Railroad, as well as the town of Colorado Springs.

MEEKER AND THE UTES

The new state faced old problems. Conflicts between white settlers and Native Americans broke out again in the 1870s. In 1878, Nathan Meeker was appointed official Indian Agent to the Ute reservation along the White River. However, he had little respect for the tribe's ancient ways of life. He tried to turn the Utes, who were hunters and horse racers, into Christians and farmers.

When the Utes became hostile to his ideas, Meeker called in army troops for protection. The Utes, fearful of the United States government, saw this as a threat. They killed Meeker and kidnapped his wife and daughters.

Upon hearing the news, white settlers who wanted the Ute's land were outraged. "The Utes Must Go!" became a battle cry. To avenge the

Many settlers feared being attacked by the Ute and fled from their homes.

attack, the United States army invaded the Ute reservation, killing 37 Utes. The Utes also lost much of their land. In 1881, the government moved them to small reservations in Utah and southern Colorado. Today, the reservations are called the Ute Mountain and Southern Ute reservations.

WHO'S WHO IN COLORADO?

Chief Ouray (1833–1880) was leader of the Colorado Ute during the mid-1800s. He spoke English, Spanish, and two Native American languages. He worked hard for peace between whites and the Ute, and negotiated several treaties with the United States government on behalf of the Ute. Today he is considered one of the Ute's greatest leaders.

Miners built tunnels into the mountainsides to search for gold and silver.

SILVER AND GOLD

In 1878, silver was discovered in Leadville, Colorado. The discovery started a mining boom that made people rich almost overnight. The most famous silver baron in Colorado was Horace Tabor. Tabor's "Matchless Mine" near Leadville produced more than $10 million worth of silver. People began calling him the "Silver King." Tabor enjoyed showing off his wealth. He used a portion of it to build opera houses in Leadville and Denver, as well as a huge mansion for his young wife, Elizabeth "Baby" Doe. Tabor became so popular that the people of Colorado later elected him to be their lieutenant governor.

The silver boom didn't last long. In 1893, the price of silver fell. Some mines were forced to shut down. Many silver miners lost their jobs, and other businesses in Colorado suffered because few people could afford to buy their products. Even Horace Tabor went broke. He died, penniless, in 1899. His wife, Baby Doe, promised to keep working the Matchless Mine, even though there was little silver left to mine. For 36 years she lived in a broken-down shack outside the Matchless Mine, where she froze to death in winter 1935.

A gold boom soon helped replace the failing silver mining industry. In 1891, a cowboy named Bob Womack struck gold near the town of Cripple Creek. The town soon became one of the largest producers of gold in the United States. Over the next twenty years, miners dug out between $15 million and $20 million a year in gold from the mountains.

LABOR STRIKES

Mining may have helped make the state rich, but it also brought many problems. In the early part of the twentieth century, tensions erupted between miners and mine owners. Mining was dangerous, and the pay was low. Dynamite was used to blast tunnels, which then sometimes collapsed. Accidents and deaths were frequent. In the early 1900s, miners began demanding more pay and safer working conditions. However, mine owners refused to listen, and as a result many miners formed organizations called unions. Union members banded together so they had more power to bargain with mine owners.

Mine owners did all they could to stop the unions. Tensions reached a peak in 1913, when union coal miners in the town of Ludlow went on strike and refused to work. Colorado Governor Elias Ammons called in the state militia to break the strike. On April 20, 1914, militiamen began shooting on the worker's tents, and set fire to the tent city. A number of people died in the massacre, including some women and children who suffocated in underground pits they had dug under their

In the early 1900s, miners tried to negotiate better pay and safer working conditions by going on strike.

tent. After what became known as the "Ludlow Massacre," President Woodrow Wilson sent in federal troops to help bring peace to the town. However, stikes continued in Colorado for years to come.

MONEYMAKERS

In 1914, World War I (1914–1918) broke out in Europe. The United States joined the war in 1917 to help the British and the French. About 43,000 Coloradans joined the armed forces and went to fight overseas.

Colorado's mining products played a role in helping to win the war. Small oil fields had been drilled in Colorado many years before, but the demand for oil during wartime turned it into a big business. Oil was desperately needed to fuel planes, trains, tanks, and trucks for troops overseas. Also, people throughout the country were beginning to buy automobiles, which needed oil to run. Oil became so valuable that people called it "black gold."

Troops overseas also needed food, and Colorado's farmers were happy to provide it. Farmers grew more and more crops to help feed hungry soldiers. With demand for their crops at an all-time high, Colorado farmers made more money than ever.

After the war, the growth of railroads helped farmers get even more of their crops to market. In 1927, the Moffat railroad tunnel was built through the Rocky Mountains, helping farmers to transport their crops across the Rockies faster than ever before.

The scenic beauty of the Rocky Mountains also brought money into Colorado. In 1915, President Woodrow Wilson created the 358-square-mile (928-sq-km) Rocky Mountain National Park. The park soon attracted visitors from all over the world.

RACIAL UNREST

In the 1920s, problems erupted between African Americans and whites in Colorado. After the Civil War, a group called the Ku Klux Klan (KKK) was formed in the southern states. This "brotherhood" of white Protes-

Benjamin Stapleton served five terms as mayor of Denver. His hold on power, backed by a political machine tied to business interests as well as the KKK, ended with the election of reformer J. Quigg Newton.

tants hated people who were not white and Protestant. They harassed and sometimes murdered African Americans as well as Jews, Roman Catholics, and Hispanics.

The KKK had a great deal of influence in Colorado in the early 1900s. In 1923, group member Benjamin Stapleton was elected mayor of Denver. The following year, the KKK helped elect Colorado's governor and a United States senator. The KKK had a hold on Colorado politics and intimidated anyone who disagreed with them. Over time, however, the Klan's horrible acts of violence turned the people of Colorado against them, and their power gradually disappeared.

THE GREAT DEPRESSION AND WORLD WAR II

The Great Depression (1929–1939) began in 1929 when the stock market crashed. People all over the United States lost huge amounts of money when the value of their investments plummeted. Many people had a hard time buying food and other necessities. Businesses couldn't sell their products, and many of them closed, leaving thousands of people out of work. The United States government tried to help by creating the Civilian Conservation Corps (CCC), an organization that employed people to build roads, parks, and other public works.

Colorado, like the rest of the country, was greatly affected. Banks closed and factories shut down. Thousands of people in Colorado lost their jobs and homes.

To make matters worse, a drought struck the Great Plains region during the 1930s. Much of Colorado's soil dried up and blew away. Very few crops would grow. Colorado was one of several states in a region that became known as the "Dust Bowl." The Dust Bowl suffered severe dust storms that blanketed even the insides of houses with powdery soil. Many people left Colorado, hoping to find a better life in places like California.

Many CCC workers were put to work planting trees in Colorado.

The Great Depression gradually came to an end with the start of World War II (1939–1945). The United States entered the war on December 8, 1941, after Japan bombed Pearl Harbor, a U.S. Naval base in Hawaii. About 140,000 people from Colorado joined the United States armed forces to fight in Europe and in the Pacific.

FAMOUS FIRSTS

- The first national park designed to preserve relics and artifacts of a people's culture was Mesa Verde National Park, 1906
- The first commercial ski area opened for business in Aspen, 1947

During the war, demand for Colorado's mining and agricultural products skyrocketed. Once again, Colorado's economy was running at full steam. The government set up several air bases in Colorado. Factories such as the Denver Ordnance Plant were built to make guns and ammunition. Because most men were away fighting, women worked in these factories. Manufacturing grew to such an extent that it replaced agriculture as Colorado's most important industry.

INDUSTRIES ON THE RISE

The war also influenced another industry in Colorado—tourism. During the war, the United States Army trained "ski troops" in Colorado. When the war was over, some soldiers returned to Colorado's Rocky Mountains and opened ski resorts. Peter Seibert and Earl Eaton, ski troopers from the 10th Mountain Division, turned Vail into a resort town. In 1947, Walter and Elizabeth Paepke started a ski resort in Aspen. They bought a 3-mile (5-km) ski lift, which was the longest and fastest ski lift in the world at that time. By the 1960s, Colorado had become one of the world's most popular ski areas.

The military industry also continued to be important in Colorado. Shortly after World War II, Colorado played a key role in what became known as "the Cold War." It was not a shooting war, but a bitter rivalry between the United States and another country, the Soviet Union. Both countries feared one another, and built deadly bombs for protection. Atomic bombs were made from a silvery-white metal

NORAD is a military defense operation located in the Cheyenne Mountain complex outside Colorado Springs.

called uranium, which was discovered in great quantities in southern Colorado. Factories were built near Durango to process uranium.

In 1958, the United States Air Force opened a training academy for young pilots in Colorado Springs. The headquarters of the North American Air Defense Command combat operations center was located near Colorado Springs. Its job was to guard against air attacks from the Soviet Union. The center, now called the North American Aerospace Defense Command (NORAD), was completed in 1966. It lies 1,200 feet (366 m) underground inside of Cheyenne Mountain. The building itself sits on giant springs to protect it (allowing it to sway up to 12 inches/30 cm) during an earthquake or explosion.

In later years, several defense companies moved to Colorado, including the Martin Marietta Aerospace Corporation. These companies made rockets, missiles, and other defense weapons. Other high-technology companies also came to Colorado to make electronic and scientific equipment.

GROWTH AND CHANGE

New businesses have helped make Colorado one of the fastest growing states in the country. Between 1950 and 1975, the state's population more than tripled to 4.3 million.

As more people and businesses came to Colorado, the need for water increased. Colorado is generally quite dry, and most of the water supply is in the western part of the state. To address this problem, dams were built along Colorado's rivers. These dams carry water through the Rocky Mountains to the dry plains and cities of eastern Colorado. They also fuel power plants that provide energy for Coloradans.

However, the dams have also created problems. There are so many dams on the Colorado River that all the river's water is used along the way. Hardly any water reaches the Gulf of California, where the river empties out. Today, Colorado and neighboring states continually debate how to "share" the water so that everyone gets enough.

Pollution from defense plants was another big problem. In the 1970s, it was discovered that deadly chemicals were leaking into the ground from the Rocky Mountain Arsenal, which was built to produce chemical weapons. As a result, the soil and groundwater around the plant was contaminated with dangerous pollutants. The plant was shut down, and a massive cleanup began in the 1980s. The arsenal site is now used as a national wildlife refuge. Similar problems were also found at Rocky Flats, a former nuclear weapons plant outside of Denver. This site is also undergoing environmental cleanup.

Growth has also created other problems. The scenic Rocky Mountains are a big draw for visitors, and there are more ski resorts in Colorado than ever before. Although this rapid growth brings more money into Colorado, it is also polluting the state's water and air. Some people fear that growth will disrupt wildlife and animal habitats. In 1998, a group of protesters set fire to a building at Vail's ski resort to protest Vail's planned expansion. The protestors believed the expansion would destroy the state's dwindling population of lynxes, a type of wildcat that lives in Colorado. The fire caused $12 million in damage, but ultimately had little effect—Vail's new ski resort opened in January 2000.

In April 1999, a tragic event ripped apart Columbine High School in Littleton, a suburb of Denver. Two students, Eric Harris and Dylan Klebold, stormed into their high school with firearms, killing twelve students and one teacher before killing themselves. Twenty-three people were injured. It was one of the deadliest school killings in the United States.

FIND OUT MORE

How are scientists and environmental groups working to clean up rivers and waterways in Colorado?

Students and families gather at a memorial for those killed in the Columbine shooting.

Despite these problems, Colorado is well known for its high quality of life, and continues to attract people and businesses. Denver is a center for communications and high tech businesses. Denver suburbs (places just outside the city of Denver) are spreading out far and wide. In the 1990s, Douglas County, south of Denver, was the fastest growing county in the entire United States.

The leaders of Colorado are finding ways to meet the unique challenges of their state. In May 2000, Governor Bill Owens established the Commission on Saving Open Spaces, Farms, and Ranches. Its members are looking for ways to protect the state's natural landscapes. Nearly everyone, it seems, wants to make sure that future generations will be able to enjoy Colorado's scenic wonders.

CHAPTER FOUR

GOVERNING COLORADO

Colorado's state government is organized according to the state's constitution. A constitution is an official document that defines the way in which the government will be run. Colorado's constitution was adopted in 1876 and is still used today. However, it has been amended, or changed, several times. Voters must approve all amendments to the constitution in an election.

Colorado's constitution divides the state government into three parts, or branches: legislative, executive, and judicial. No one branch has more power than any other. These three branches work together to govern Colorado.

The capitol building, which was begun in 1890, took almost twenty years to complete.

EXECUTIVE BRANCH

The executive branch makes sure that state laws are carried out and enforced. The governor heads the executive branch. The people of Colorado elect the governor, who serves a four-year term and can be re-elected only once.

The governor plays an important role in making and carrying out laws. He or she helps the legislature (Colorado's lawmaking body) decide how to spend the state's money. Governors also act as head of the state militia, or military forces. He or she can call the militia into action in case of an emergency.

The governor doesn't work alone. The lieutenant governor, secretary of state, attorney general, and treasurer assist the governor. They are also elected to four-year terms and can be reelected only once. The governor also oversees sixteen departments in the executive branch, such as the departments of agriculture, human services, education, transportation, and many others.

LEGISLATIVE BRANCH

The legislative branch makes the state's laws. New laws may apply to subject areas such as education, finance, or local government. The legislature also decides how the state's money will be spent, allocating it among schools, roads, and other things that the state needs.

Colorado calls its state legislature the General Assembly. The General Assembly

COLORADO GOVERNORS

Name	Term	Name	Term
John L. Routt	1876–1879	Julius C. Gunter	1917–1919
Frederick W. Pitkin	1879–1883	Oliver H. Shoup	1919–1923
James B. Grant	1883–1885	William E. Sweet	1923–1925
Benjamin H. Eaton	1885–1887	Clarence J. Morley	1925–1927
Alva Adams	1887–1889	William H. Adams	1927–1933
Job A. Cooper	1889–1891	Edwin C. Johnson	1933–1937
John L. Routt	1891–1893	Ray H. Talbot	1937
Davis H. Waite	1893–1895	Teller Ammons	1937–1939
Albert W. McIntire	1895–1897	Ralph L. Carr	1939–1943
Alva Adams	1897–1899	John C. Vivian	1943–1947
Charles S. Thomas	1899–1901	William L. Knous	1947–1950
James B. Orman	1901–1903	Walter W. Johnson	1950–1951
James H. Peabody	1903–1905	Daniel I. J. Thornton	1951–1955
Alva Adams	1905	Edwin C. Johnson	1955–1957
James H. Peabody	1905	Stephen L. R. McNichols	1957–1963
Jesse F. McDonald	1905–1907	John A. Love	1963–1973
Henry A. Buchtel	1907–1909	John D. Vanderhoof	1973–1975
John F. Shafroth	1909–1913	Richard D. Lamm	1975–1987
Elias M. Ammons	1913–1915	Roy R. Romer	1987–1999
George A. Carlson	1915–1917	Bill Owens	1999–2007
		Bill Ritter	2007–

lower court, they can request to have it reviewed by the court of appeals. The court of appeals is made up of sixteen judges.

Colorado's highest court is the supreme court. The supreme court is made up of one chief justice (judge) and six associate justices. The governor appoints all the justices.

A group of private citizens, called a commission, nominates (picks) supreme court justices for appointment by the governor. After serving for two years, a judge must be elected by Colorado voters. If elected, a justice serves a ten-year term.

TAKE A TOUR OF DENVER, THE STATE CAPITAL

Denver is Colorado's largest city. It is often called the "Queen City of the Plains" because it is the cultural, shopping, and entertainment capital of the region. In fact, so many people have discovered its appeal that it is one of the fastest growing cities in the United States. According to the 2000 Census, more than 554,600 people live in Denver. The area surrounding Denver, called the Denver metropolitan area, also has a large number of residents. In 2000, the counties of Adams, Arapahoe, Denver, Douglas, and Jefferson had a total of 2,109,282 people.

One of the most beautiful buildings in Denver is the Colorado state capitol, built in the 1890s. To commemorate the state's gold rush days, the capitol dome is covered with 200 ounces (5,670 grams) of gold that

was mined in Colorado. Rose onyx, a rare stone found only in Colorado, lines the inside walls of the capitol.

To see Colorado state senators and representatives at work, have a seat in the visitors' gallery on the third floor. Or, you can walk up 93 steps into the dome to see amazing views of the Rocky Mountains. On a clear day, you can see from Pikes Peak to the Wyoming border. Before you leave the capitol, take a minute to stand on the fifteenth step of the capitol building. At 5,280 feet (1,610 m) above sea level, this step is exactly one mile high. Not surprisingly, another one of Denver's nicknames is the "Mile High City."

The Denver skyline sparkles at twilight.

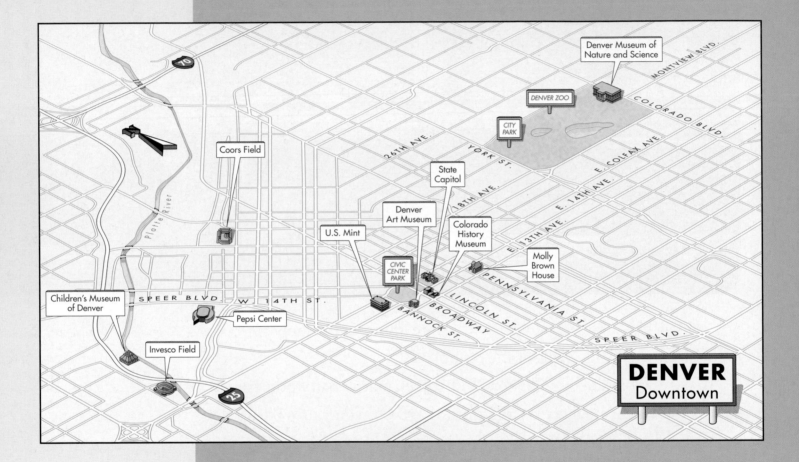

Denver Museum of Nature and Science

DENVER ZOO

CITY PARK

Coors Field

State Capitol

Denver Art Museum

Colorado History Museum

U.S. Mint

CIVIC CENTER PARK

Molly Brown House

Children's Museum of Denver

Pepsi Center

Invesco Field

Platte River

SPEER BLVD.

W. 14TH ST.

BANNOCK ST.

BROADWAY

LINCOLN ST.

PENNSYLVANIA ST.

26TH AVE.

YORK ST.

18TH AVE.

E. 13TH AVE.

E. 14TH AVE.

E. COLFAX AVE.

SPEER BLVD.

MONTVIEW BLVD.

COLORADO BLVD.

DENVER
Downtown

Two blocks west of the capitol is Civic Center Park. The park has colorful flower gardens. Plays and concerts are often performed at the park's open-air theater.

No trip to Denver would be complete without a visit to the United States Mint. This is one of the places where the United States government makes coins. The Denver Mint strikes eight billion coins a year—about thirty million coins a day! Each coin minted in Denver has a small D stamped on it. You can take a tour of the mint, or watch a video in the visitors' gallery, to see how coins are minted, bagged, sorted, and counted.

The Molly Brown House in downtown Denver is a historic landmark. Margaret "Molly" Tobin Brown was on the famous ship *Titanic* when it sank in 1912. Molly survived and helped other people to safety. "I'm unsinkable!" she exclaimed. Today, her house has displays about Denver and the Brown family history.

If you enjoy history, take a tour of the Colorado History Museum, where photographs, news clippings, and artifacts tell the story of Colorado. Denver's Four Mile Historic Park is a living history museum. This 14-acre (6-hectare) farm is run just like a farm from the mid-1800s. On the weekends, visitors can take a ride in a stagecoach.

The Children's Museum of Denver is a great place for children of all ages. There are lots of fun hands-on exhibits at the museum. You can build a car and test drive it. There's also a woodworking shop where you can use tools to make your own masterpiece. When you're done, take a stroll up to the 16th Street mall and Larimer Square, where there are lots of shops and restaurants.

Denver is also the site of the National Western Stock Show and Rodeo, the largest rodeo and stock show in the world. Professional cowboys and cowgirls from across the country ride bucking

Molly Brown is famous for surviving the sinking of the *Titanic*, and for her role in organizing rescue efforts.

EXTRA! EXTRA!

What became known as the "Denver Mint" robbery occurred in 1922, just a few days before Christmas. Thieves stole $200,000 from a bank delivery truck making a pickup at the Denver Mint. Although police determined that seven people may have been involved in the robbery, no one was ever charged with the crime.

broncos and lasso calves. The show also displays the region's best livestock.

If you're a sports fan, Denver is the place for you. The Colorado Rockies baseball team plays at Coors Field. The Pepsi Center is home to the Denver Nuggets basketball team and the Colorado Avalanche hockey team. The Denver Broncos play football at Invesco Field at Mile High.

The Colorado Avalanche hockey team won the Stanley Cup in 2001.

CHAPTER FIVE

THE PEOPLE AND PLACES OF COLORADO

Colorado's mountainous landscape, powdery snow, and well-known resorts attract many skiers each year.

According to the 2000 Census, Colorado is home to 4,301,261 people. Colorado's population is booming. In the last ten years, the state's population has grown by more than one million people. It is the third-fastest growing state behind Nevada and Arizona.

Most people in Colorado live in cities along the eastern slope of the Rockies. These "Front Range" cities include Denver, Colorado Springs, Castle Rock, Fort Collins, Boulder, Pueblo, and several others.

MEET THE PEOPLE

People of all backgrounds have made their home in Colorado. About eight of every ten people in Colorado are of European descent. Almost four of every hundred are African-American, two of every hundred are Asian, and one in every hundred Coloradans is Native American.

A Ute man plays a flute on the Ute reservation in southwest Colorado.

Colorado also has one of the largest and fastest growing Hispanic populations in the country. More than 735,000 people from a Spanish-speaking background live in Colorado. Festive Mexican murals decorate Denver, and every spring the city hosts Cinco de Mayo, or "fifth of May," festival to celebrate Mexico's victory over the French at the Battle of Puebla on May 5, 1862.

Education is important to the people of Colorado. There are many public colleges and universities in the state, including Colorado State University in Fort Collins, and the University of Colorado in Boulder, Denver, and Colorado Springs. The United States Air Force Academy is in Colorado Springs. Many small two-year community colleges are also located throughout the state.

FIND OUT MORE

In the 1500s, nearly everyone in Colorado was Native American. Today, only 1 in every 100 people is Native American. Trace the decline in Colorado's Native American population over the last six hundred years. Create a graph that illustrates your finding.

WORKING IN COLORADO

The largest number of people, about 225,000, work in service industries. These are businesses that provide services people need, such as banks, law offices, hospitals, shops, and insurance companies. The United States government also employs many workers in Colorado. More people work for the United States government in Denver than in any other city except Washington, D.C.

Many jobs in the service industry are related to tourism, which plays a major role in the Colorado economy. Western Colorado's economy, in particular, depends largely on visitors who come to the Rocky Mountains to ski and shop. People who work in tourism hold jobs at places such as hotels, ski resorts, and car rental companies.

Manufacturing is Colorado's second-largest industry. More than 173,000 people work in manufacturing. Colorado is a leading producer of computer and electronic equipment. One of the state's largest employers, Lockheed Martin, makes rockets, as well as other military and scientific equipment.

Food processing is also an important manufacturing activity. Many Colorado companies package and process meat and vegetables for sale in stores. Colorado brews more beer than any other state except Texas. The Coors Brewery in Golden is the largest brewery on a single site in the world.

Cherries—along with peaches, grapes, apricots, and apples—are grown successfully on the western slope (west of the Continental Divide) in Colorado. Ask an adult for help making the recipe below. When you're done, you'll find out why it is called "Cherries in the Snow."

CHERRIES IN THE SNOW

2 8-oz. packages cream cheese, softened
4 cups nondairy whipped topping
1 tsp. vanilla
angel food cake, crumbled
1-2 cans cherry pie filling

1. Combine cream cheese, whipped topping, and vanilla in large mixing bowl.
2. Place half of cream cheese mixture in a 9 x 11 glass baking dish.
3. Sprinkle angel food cake over mixture.
4. Cover angel food cake with other half of mixture.
5. Top with cherry pie filling.
6. Allow to cool in refrigerator for 1–2 hours until firm.

Aside from beef cattle, some farmers raise sheep on ranches in Colorado.

About 11,000 Coloradans work on farms and ranches. Farms along the Arkansas and South Platte Rivers grow sugar beets, beans, and other vegetables. Farmers in the Colorado River Valley are known for growing some of the tastiest peaches, apples, and cherries in the world. Farmers also raise sheep and horses as well as beef cattle, which is one of Colorado's most important farm products.

Mining still brings money into Colorado, although today, machines do most of the hard work. About 15,000 people work in mining. Oil, natural gas, and coal are Colorado's most valuable mining products. Gold and silver are still mined as well, along with molybdenum, which is used to harden steel.

TAKE A TOUR OF COLORADO

Eastern Colorado

Let's start our tour of the Centennial State on the wide-open plains of eastern Colorado. In La Junta, the Koshare Indian Museum has more than $10 million worth of Native American art and artifacts on display, including jewelry, beads, and baskets. The Kiva Trading Post inside the museum offers authentic Native American items for sale.

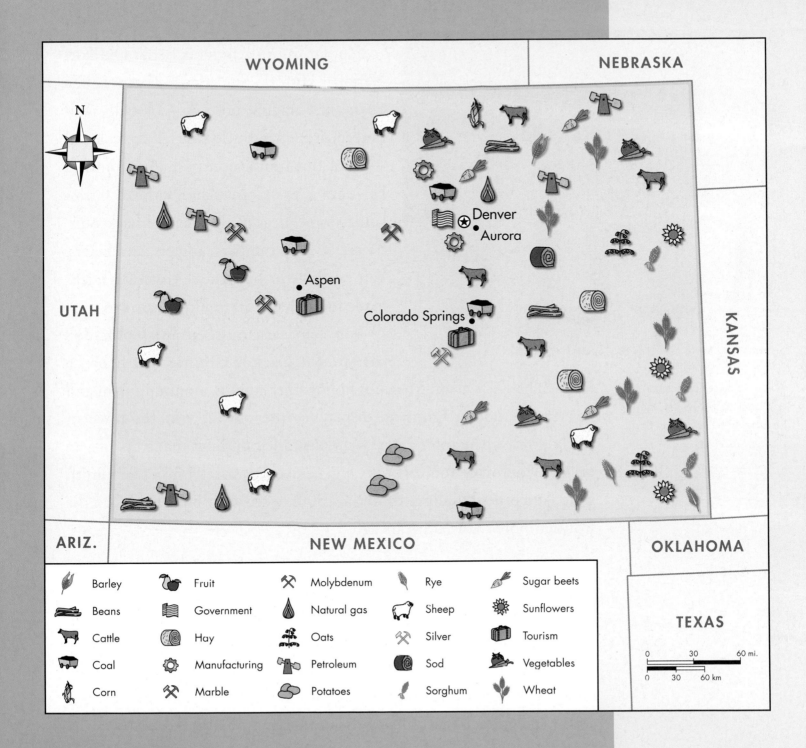

WYOMING

NEBRASKA

N

UTAH

KANSAS

ARIZ.

NEW MEXICO

OKLAHOMA

Aspen

Denver
Aurora

Colorado Springs

TEXAS

	Barley		Fruit		Molybdenum		Rye		Sugar beets
	Beans		Government		Natural gas		Sheep		Sunflowers
	Cattle		Hay		Oats		Silver		Tourism
	Coal		Manufacturing		Petroleum		Sod		Vegetables
	Corn		Marble		Potatoes		Sorghum		Wheat

0   30   60 mi.
0   30   60 km

A visit to Bent's Fort takes you back to the 1840s, the heyday of activity at the Fort.

Not far from La Junta is Bent's Old Fort National Historic Site. Bent's Fort was one of the first trading posts in Colorado. Volunteers dressed in buckskins tell the colorful story of this frontier outpost. Just south of La Junta is the Comanche National Grasslands. Some areas of this remote backcountry are open to campers, anglers, and hikers. You can hike or bike to see dinosaur tracks made more than 150 million years ago.

You can learn more about Colorado's past in Kit Carson County north of La Junta. The Kit Carson Museum honors this famous mountain man and has his six-shooter (gun) on display. Farther north, visit the town of Burlington, where more than twenty historic buildings make up an area called Old Town. You can tour a general store, a saloon, a blacksmith shop, and other buildings from the 1800s to see what life was like on the frontier more than 100 years ago.

Central Colorado

One of the most impressive natural attractions in Colorado is Royal Gorge in Cañon City. The gorge was formed over a period of three thousand years by the Arkansas River, which cut a channel deep into the mountains. The world's highest suspension bridge, Royal Gorge Bridge, crosses the gorge. You can walk or drive across the bridge, or cross the gorge on a tram. If you're looking for more adventure, take a raft trip down the white waters of the Arkansas River below.

Southeast of Cañon City is the city of Pueblo, home to the annual Colorado State Fair. In downtown Pueblo, the El Pueblo Museum has interesting exhibits about Native Americans and mountain men who once lived in the area.

Next let's tour the Front Range cities of central Colorado. Boulder, northwest of Denver, was named for its large rocks. Boulder is also home to the main campus of the state's largest university, the University of Colorado. More than 26,000 students attend the school, which was founded in 1876.

At Boulder's Fiske Planetarium you can take a tour of our solar system. An organization called the National Center for Atmospheric Research in Boulder studies the earth's weather patterns. Computers, weather balloons, and satellites help to create models that can simulate, or reproduce, the climate anywhere in the world.

Another major city in Colorado is Fort Collins, located north of Denver. Fort Collins is the fifth-largest city in Colorado. It is home to Colorado State University, one of the top universities in the country. Sometimes called "The Choice City," Fort Collins offers lots of choices in terms of recreation—the city has numerous art galleries, restaurants, and performing arts centers, as well as outdoor activities such as hiking and biking.

South of Fort Collins are two other big cities, Loveland and Longmont. Loveland is well-known for its commitment to the arts. Every

The sandstone rock formations in the Garden of the Gods are more than 300 million years old.

summer the city hosts a sculpture show that is enjoyed by thousands of art lovers from around the state. Many artists live and work in the city's historic downtown area. The nearby city of Longmont was founded in 1871 and was named in honor of Longs Peak, which is clearly visible from town. To learn more about the history of the Longmont area check out the Longmont Museum, where you'll find exhibits about the region's early settlers.

Colorado Springs is the state's second-largest city after Denver. One of Colorado Springs' most popular attractions is a giant "garden" of red rocks called the Garden of the Gods. According to ancient Ute legend, these rocks were once giants, but because they invaded Ute lands the Great Spirit turned them to stone.

The United States Air Force Academy has exhibits of early aircraft and offers self-guided tours. You might be lucky enough to see student pilots practicing landings and takeoffs. Colorado Springs is also home to the United States Olympic Training Complex, where young Olympic athletes train.

FIND OUT MORE

In 1893, professor and poet Katharine Lee Bates climbed to the top of Pikes Peak. The view was so awe-inspiring that she wrote a poem called "America the Beautiful." The poem was soon set to music and became one of America's most beloved songs. Today, many Americans believe that it should be our national anthem. Find out why.

Just west of Colorado Springs is Colorado's most famous mountain, Pikes Peak. You can ride a cog railway or drive in a car to the summit. Or simply walk around and enjoy the mountain air and the breathtaking view from the bottom.

Also west of Colorado Springs is the Manitou Cliff Dwelling, the site of a reconstructed forty-room pueblo where the Anasazi once lived. During June and August, traditional Native American dances and ceremonies are performed at the site. West of Colorado Springs, near Cripple Creek, is the Florissant Fossil Beds National Monument. About 36 million years ago, fossils of trees and animals were imprinted here when volcanoes erupted.

Rocky Mountains

Next, let's take a tour through the Rocky Mountains. Nestled in the mountains are many ski towns famous for their white, powdery snow. Vail and Aspen host the World Cup Ski Racing Competitions every year. Arapaho Mountain is the highest ski area in North America. Skiers and snowboarders also enjoy the slopes at Steamboat Springs, Winter Park, Breckenridge, and Copper Mountain.

Skiers head for the hills at Steamboat Springs.

The most popular attraction in Colorado is Rocky Mountain National Park. The park covers 265,769 acres (107,636 ha) and includes some of the most spectacular mountain views in the world. You can hike, bike, boat, or fish, and many of the park's trails are open to horseback riding. Bighorn sheep, bears, deer, and elk roam through the park. If you're lucky, you might spot a peregrine falcon, one of the world's fastest birds.

The Rockies are dotted with ghost towns such as St. Elmo and Eldora. In Colorado's early days, these towns died when the gold and silver ran out. Today, visitors can see the empty buildings left behind. The town of Leadville is a great place to relive Colorado's mining past. The National Mining Hall of Fame and Museum has working models of

At the National Mining Hall of Fame you can get a close-up look at what mining is all about.

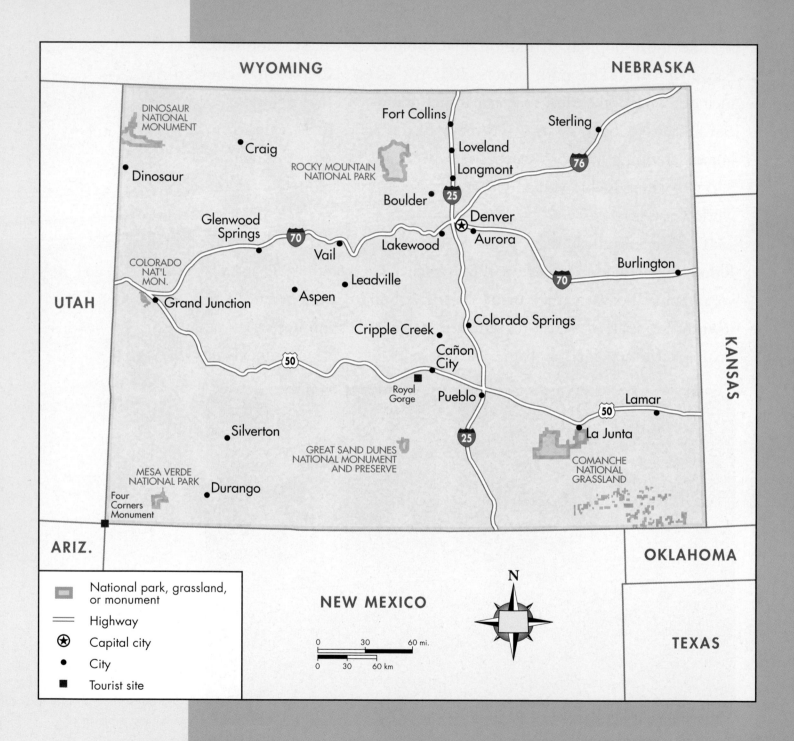

WYOMING

NEBRASKA

DINOSAUR
NATIONAL
MONUMENT

Craig

ROCKY MOUNTAIN
NATIONAL PARK

Fort Collins

Sterling

Loveland

Longmont

76

Dinosaur

Boulder

25

Glenwood
Springs

70

Denver

Vail

Lakewood

Aurora

COLORADO
NAT'L
MON.

Leadville

Burlington

70

Grand Junction

Aspen

Cripple Creek

Colorado Springs

UTAH

50

Cañon
City

KANSAS

Royal
Gorge

Pueblo

Lamar

50

Silverton

25

La Junta

GREAT SAND DUNES
NATIONAL MONUMENT
AND PRESERVE

COMANCHE
NATIONAL
GRASSLAND

MESA VERDE
NATIONAL PARK

Four
Corners
Monument

Durango

ARIZ.

OKLAHOMA

NEW MEXICO

N

TEXAS

National park, grassland,
or monument

Highway

Capital city

City

Tourist site

0   30   60 mi.

0   30   60 km

mining machines. You can also peer into Horace Tabor's Matchless Mine. Don't miss the Matchless Mine Cabin where Tabor's widow, Elizabeth "Baby Doe" Tabor, spent her last years.

Next we'll head northwest to Glenwood Springs. For hundreds of years, the Ute came here to bathe in the natural springs because they believed that the springs would cure illness. They called it Yampah Springs, which means "big medicine." Today, many people still believe in its healing power, and they come to take a quick dip in the large hot springs pool.

FIND OUT MORE

The life story of Elizabeth "Baby Doe" Tabor, wife of silver magnate Horace Tabor, became the subject of an opera called *The Ballad of Baby Doe*. It was first presented in 1956 in Central City and is one of the most performed American operas today. What is an opera and when was opera first performed? Where?

Tourists spend time in the steaming waters of the pool at Glenwood Springs.

The town of Durango, in southwestern Colorado, is home to the Durango & Silverton Narrow Gauge Railroad. Its steam engine is the most famous train in Colorado and has been operating since 1881.

Next, head east to the Great Sand Dunes National Park, where you can see the tallest sand dunes in North America. Some are at least 700 feet (213 m) tall. You can ski or sled down the dunes when they aren't covered in snow.

The tallest dunes at Great Sand Dunes National Park rise more than 700 feet (213 m).

Next we'll head down the western slope of the Rockies. About 150 million years ago, dinosaurs roamed this area. There's even a town in northwestern Colorado named Dinosaur. Real dinosaur bones can be found at nearby Dinosaur National Monument. At the Dinosaur Valley Museum in Grand Junction there are one-million-year-old fossils of dinosaurs, bugs, plants, and birds. You can also see scientists digging for dinosaur bones in nearby Rabbit Valley.

West of Grand Junction is the Colorado National Monument. This is a colorful area of steep red canyons and sandstone rock formations. East of Grand Junction is Grand Mesa, the nation's highest flat-topped mountain.

South of Grand Junction is Mesa Verde National Park. The park has some of the most amazing cliff dwellings in the southwest. They were built by the Anasazi 800 years ago. The largest, Cliff Palace, is four stories tall with more than 200 rooms.

The Ute Mountain Indian Reservation is also in southwestern Colorado. Barely a mile from the Ute reservation is the Four Corners Monument, the only place in the United States where four states meet. A flat monument marks the exact spot where Utah, Colorado, New Mexico, and Arizona come together. Each state's flag is displayed, along with the United States flag and the flags of the Navajo Nation and the Ute Tribe. A plaque at the site reads, "Four states here meet in freedom under God."

COLORADO ALMANAC

Statehood date and number: August 1, 1876/38th

State seal: At the top is the eye of God within a triangle, from which golden rays radiate on both sides. Below the eye is a scroll, the Roman fasces, and a bundle of birch or elm rods with a battle axe bound together by red thongs. Below the scroll is a shield that has three snow-capped mountains and two miner's tools (a pick and a sledgehammer). Adopted in 1877.

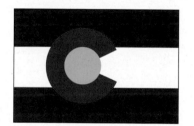

State flag: The flag consists of three alternate stripes of blue and white. A red C is slightly off center and to the left in the middle of the flag. A golden disk fills the open space inside the C. Adopted in 1911.

Geographic center: Park, 30 miles (48 km) northwest of Pikes Peak

Total area/rank: 104,094 square miles (269,601 sq km)/8th

Borders: Wyoming, Kansas, Oklahoma, New Mexico, Nebraska, and Utah

Latitude and longitude: Colorado is located approximately between 37° 00' and 41° 00' N and 102° 03' and 109° 03' W

Highest/lowest elevation: Mount Elbert, 14,431 feet (4,399 m) above sea level/Along the Arikaree River, 3,315 feet (1,010 m) above sea level

Hottest/coldest temperature: 118°F (48°C) at Bennett on July 11, 1888/–61°F (–52°C) at Maybell on February 1, 1985

Land area/rank: 103,718 square miles (268,627 sq km)/8th

Inland water area: 376 square miles (974 sq km)

Population (2000 Census): 4,301,261/24th

Population of major cities:
   Denver: 554,636
   Colorado Springs: 360,890
   Aurora: 276,393
   Lakewood: 144,126
   Fort Collins: 118,652

Origin of state name: Spanish word meaning "red-colored." Named for the Colorado River, which flows through red canyons.

State capital: Denver

Counties: 64

State government: 35 senators and 65 representatives

Major rivers/lakes: Colorado, Rio Grande, Arkansas, North Platte, South Platte, San Juan, Gunnison, Dolores Rivers/Grand Lake, Blue Mesa Reservoir, Granby Reservoir, and John Martin Reservoir

Farm products:

Milk, lettuce, cherries, pears, apples, plums, peaches, potatoes, beans, onions, barley, wheat, sugar beets, hay, corn, tomatoes, cantaloupe, and watermelons

Livestock: Beef cattle and sheep

Manufactured products: Rockets, spacecraft, medical supplies, beer, computers and office equipment, televisions, clothing, lumber and furniture, books, pottery, and sporting goods

Mining products: Oil, natural gas, coal, gold, silver, molybdenum, and uranium

Animal: Rocky Mountain bighorn sheep

Bird: Lark bunting

Fair: Pueblo (August)

Fish: Greenback cutthroat trout

Flower: White and lavender columbine

Folk dance: Square dance

Fossil: Stegosaurus

Gemstone: Aquamarine

Grass: Blue grama grass

Insect: Colorado hairstreak butterfly

Motto: Nil sine Numine, Latin phrase meaning "Nothing without the Deity" ("Deity" means God or God's guidance)

Nickname: Centennial State

Song: "Where the Columbines Grow," words and music by A. J. Fynn

Tree: Colorado Blue spruce

Wildlife: Bighorn sheep, mountain goats, pronghorn antelopes, mountain lions, deer, elk, black bears, beaver, coyotes, foxes, prairie dogs, marmots, chipmunks, bobcats, lark buntings, owls, hawks, eagles, falcons, hummingbirds, rattlesnakes, and black widow spiders

TIME**LINE**

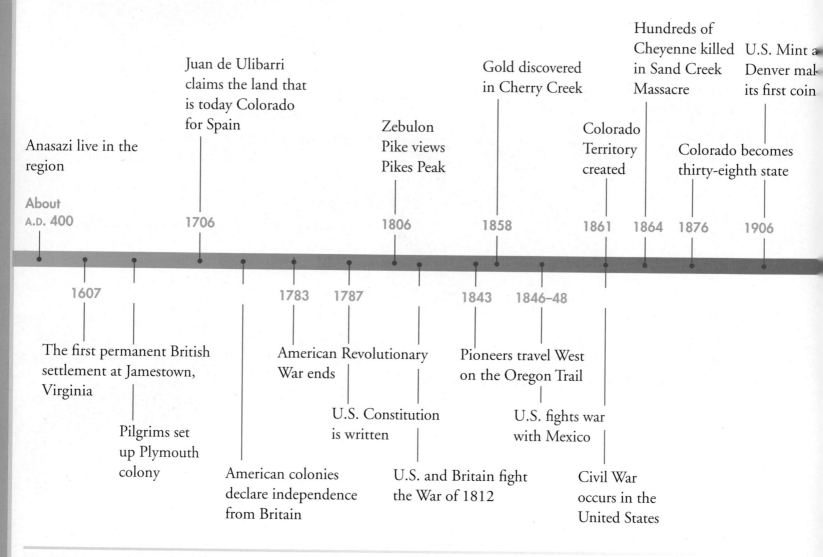

Anasazi live in the region

About A.D. 400

Juan de Ulibarri claims the land that is today Colorado for Spain

1706

Zebulon Pike views Pikes Peak

1806

Gold discovered in Cherry Creek

1858

Colorado Territory created

1861

Hundreds of Cheyenne killed in Sand Creek Massacre

1864

U.S. Mint a Denver mal its first coin

Colorado becomes thirty-eighth state

1876

1906

1607
The first permanent British settlement at Jamestown, Virginia

Pilgrims set up Plymouth colony

1783
American Revolutionary War ends

1787
U.S. Constitution is written

American colonies declare independence from Britain

U.S. and Britain fight the War of 1812

1843
Pioneers travel West on the Oregon Trail

1846–48
U.S. fights war with Mexico

Civil War occurs in the United States

Rocky Mountain National
Park established

Moffat Tunnel
opens

U.S. Air Force
Academy opens
in Colorado
Springs

NORAD completes
command center
within Cheyenne
Mountain

Frying Pan-Arkansas
River Project completed,
bringing water to eastern
Colorado

Centennial State
is 100 years old

Colorado Rockies
become first regional
major league baseball
team

1915   1927   1958   1966   1976   1985   1993

1917–18   1929   1941–45   1950–53   1964   1965–73   1969   1991   1995

U.S. takes part in
World War I

U.S. fights in
World War II

Civil rights laws
passed in the U.S.

U.S. and other nations
fight in Persian Gulf War

The stock market
crashes and U.S.
enters the Great
Depression

U.S. fights in the
Vietnam War

U.S. fights in the
Korean War

Neil Armstrong and
Edwin Aldrin land on
the moon

U.S. space
shuttle docks
with Russian
space station

GALLERY OF FAMOUS COLORADANS

Black Kettle

(?–1868)

Cheyenne chief in the mid 1800s. Black Kettle was a strong leader who tried to secure peace between white settlers and the Cheyenne. Born on the Great Plains.

Chipeta "White Singing Bird"

(1844–1924)

Second wife of Ouray, chief of the Ute Indian Nation. Together with her husband, she befriended white settlers and tried make peace between the two groups. She may have also played a role in rescuing hostages that were held by a group of Utes during the Meeker incident. Grew up near Conejos.

M. Scott Carpenter

(1925–)

Astronaut and aquanaut. In 1962 he piloted Aurora 7, orbiting the earth three times. Three years later he spent 30 days living and working on the ocean floor off the coast of California as part of an experiment. Born in Boulder.

William Harrison (Jack) Dempsey

(1895–1983)

World heavyweight boxing champion and a major sports figure in the 1920s. Born in Manassa.

Federico Peña

(1947–)

First Hispanic mayor of Denver, an office he served from 1983 to 1991 with great success. In 1993 President Clinton appointed him Secretary of Transportation. Born in Texas and lives in Denver.

Florence Rena Sabin

(1871–1953)

One of the first female professors at Johns Hopkins University and first woman to be elected to life membership in the National Academy of Sciences. In 1947 she was instrumental in the passing of several health reform bills in Colorado. Born in Central City.

Byron Raymond White

(1917–2002)

United States Supreme Court Justice. He was appointed by President Kennedy in 1962 and served until 1993. Born in Fort Collins.

GLOSSARY

ancient: very old, relating to times long past

capital: city that serves as the seat of government

capitol: building where the government meets

climate: general or average weather conditions of a region over a long period of time

colony: group of people who settle in a faraway land and are governed by their native country

constitution: laws by which a nation is organized

economy: exchange of goods and services, such as money, management, or labor

fossil: remains of an animal or plant that lived long ago, often found in layers of rock

gorge: deep, narrow passage with steep, rocky sides that was usually carved out by a stream

legislature: branch of government that makes laws

mesa: flat-topped mountain with steep sides

plateau: high, level piece of land

plain: large expanse of flat dry land, usually with few trees

population: number of people living in a certain location

reservoir: artificial (manmade) lake in which water is collected and held by a river dam

secede: to withdraw from membership in a state or federation

tourism: business of providing services such as food, lodging, and entertainment for visitors

treaty: formal, signed agreement

tributary: river that feeds a larger river or lake

FOR MORE INFORMATION

Web sites

Colorado State Government

http://www.colorado.gov

The official state government Web site, with links to tourism and recreation and information about businesses and services.

Rocky Mountain National Park

http://www.nps.gov/romo/siteindex.htm

Information about the park, including maps from the National Park Service

Denver Convention and Visitors Bureau

http://www.denver.org/

Provides information about all aspects of Denver, including maps and facts.

Books

Arnold, Caroline. *The Ancient Cliff Dwellers of Mesa Verde.* New York, NY: Houghton Mifflin, 2000.

Green, Carl R. and William R. Sanford. *Kit Carson: Frontier Scout (Legendary Heroes of the Wild West).* Berkeley Heights, NJ: Enslow Publishers, 1996.

Simon, Charnan. *Molly Brown: Sharing Her Good Fortune (Community Builders).* Danbury, CT: Children's Press, 2000.

Addresses

Governor of Colorado

136 State Capitol
Denver, CO 80203-1792

Colorado Historical Society

1300 Broadway
Denver, CO 80203

INDEX

ABOUT THE AUTHOR

Amy Miller is a writer and editor living in New York City. She has written articles and plays for children about many different subjects. To write this book about the Centennial State, she read many books and articles about Colorado.

Photographs © 2009: AP Images/Ed Andrieski: 44; Branson Reynolds: 10, 55, 70 top; Brown Brothers: 23, 63; Colorado Historical Society: 34, 56; Corbis Images: 13 (Craig Aurness), 3 right, 14 (Tom Bean), 58 (Michael Lewis), 15 (David Muench), 53 (Reuters Newmedia Inc.), 43, 46 background (Bill Ross), 52 (UPI), 29 (Baldwin H. Ward), 22, 31 top, 37, 74 bottom right, 74 top left, 74 top right, 74 bottom left; Culver Pictures: 30; Dembinsky Photo Assoc./Willard Clay: 68; Denver Public Library, Western History Collection: 26 (Colorado Historical Society/Denver Art Museum), 36 (Harry Rhoads); Folio, Inc.: 62 (Walter Bibikow), 51 (Richard Cummins); Getty Images: 49 (Glen Allison/Stone), 9 (Terry Donnelly/Stone), 4 (David Hiser/Stone), 3 left, 64 (Marc Muench/Stone), cover (Larry Ulrich/Stone); MapQuest.com, Inc.: 70 bottom left; North Wind Picture Archives: 19, 24, 25; Photo Researchers, NY/Jeff Lepore: 71 top right; Richardson Photography/Jim Richardson: 67; Robertstock.com: 16 (J. Blank), 45 (Wendell Metzen), 71 bottom right (J. Patton); Still Media: 41 (Jeffrey Aaronson), 39 (Paul Chesley), 54 (Peter Hammond), 11, 65 (David Hiser), 7 (John Russell); Stock Montage, Inc.: 27 (Theodore R. Davis), 21, 31 bottom, 32; Tom Till Photography, Inc.: 18; Visuals Unlimited: 71 left (Wally Eberhart), 70 bottom right (Jeff Greenberg), 60 (Nancy M. Wells).